AT THE edge OF light

AT THE edge OF light

Poems of

Suffering and Grief,

Life and Hope

SHARI BRASE-SMITH, RN, MS

credo
house publishers

Published in the United States of America by Credo House Publishers,
a division of Credo Communications, LLC, Grand Rapids, Michigan
credohousepublishers.com

ISBN: 978-1-62586-342-3

Cover and interior design by Sharon VanLoozenoord
Editing by Elizabeth Banks

Printed in the United States of America
First edition

Contents

Aging

Who Do You See?

What do you see when you look at me?
What words come to your mind to describe what you see?
Do you see an old woman, disabled, of no use?
Look closer, for your eyes have been deceived

My body may be old
My body may be broken
My body may carry many scars
But my body is only a shell

My shell has protected me
My shell absorbed many blows for me
My body endured violence and repeated trauma
My body has become deformed in man's eyes

But I am not my body
My spirit lives a different life
My spirit dances among the clouds
My spirit sings beautiful songs with the angels

My body may have difficulty moving
But my spirit soars freely
My body may appear wrinkled and worn
But my spirit laughs loudly at the world's definition
     of beauty

You may only see my old and tattered shell
Behold! Look deeper!
See the child spirit inside me
Look beyond the ugly scars and wrinkles
Look and see the perfect beauty inside

The scars tell a story
Battles fought are recorded here
Scars show where flesh and bone once were broken and torn
Flesh and bone fought and won to once again be made whole
Scars are like medals awarded for battles won

You may only see ugly scars
But God sees something different
You may see a life of no value
But God sees a priceless treasure

Like a caterpillar turning into a butterfly
This old woman is soon to break free
Once crawling hopelessly on the ground
Soon free to fly among the stars of the universe

Look beyond the old woman's body
See the child spirit living inside
Look beyond the brokenness

See the breathtaking beauty inside
Look beyond the physical pain and disability
See the radiant joy inside

God sees me as His treasure
Shiny, sparkly, radiant, and priceless
God sees a beloved daughter
Precious and lovely beyond words

I began life like a blob of carbon
Life's intense heat and pressure created my rough form
Life's hardships served to cut and polish me
Now my radiant beauty is about to burst forth like
    a priceless diamond
God designed me
God molded and shaped me
God allowed life's heat and pressure to purify me
God knows my true worth

Next time you look at me
What will you see?
Will you see the old broken me?
Will you see as the world sees?

Or will you see the beautiful butterfly in flight?
Or the priceless diamond shimmering in every direction?
Or the precious daughter of the Almighty?
What are you willing to see?

What about you?
Who lives inside your body?
Who does God see when He looks at you?
Do you see the child of God that you are?

Look closely, dear one
Find yourself in the loving eyes of God
See the real you, the one of highest value

See your true value, the true you.
I found the true me
Now you find the true you

Suffering

Suffering

Pain wakes me
Pain torments me
Pain never leaves me

Feet on fire
Shoulders on fire
Skin burns
Arms and legs throb
Joints ache

Sleep escapes me
Moans awaken me
Nighttime the most difficult for me

Burning
Stinging
Throbbing
Aching
Each trying to overwhelm me

Lord, You are my Healer!
Father, You are total love!
Agony, depart from me!

Where is the purpose in suffering?
Where is hope in the midst of agony?
Where is my healing?
Why must I suffer so?

Jesus, You understand my suffering
Jesus, You will never abandon me
Father, You love me
Holy Spirit, You comfort me

I know that God is good
I know that my faith is stronger than my circumstances
I know this will not be my existence throughout eternity
I know that even pain can be used for good

Lord, I don't understand the why of this hell
Lord, I trust You anyway
Lord, I belong to You
Lord, give me strength to endure
Lord, help me overcome

When sleep is taken from me because of pain
When the future seems long and dark
When hopelessness attempts to overtake me

I will sing Your praises
I will remember Your goodness
I will worship You
I will rejoice

Neither the first to suffer nor the last
I pray for endurance
I pray for patience

My hope is in You, Lord
My trust remains in Your goodness and mercy

I trust You, Lord
I love You, Lord
I worship You, Lord
I follow You always

Even in the midst of suffering
Especially in the midst of suffering

Nursing Home Life

Angels Watching

People gathered together
People standing alone
All in a "home"
Angels watching

Elderly
Chronically ill
Dying
Final stage of life
Angels watching

Physically challenged
Mentally challenged
Emotionally challenged
Spiritually challenged
Angels watching

Final passages
Lives lived well
Lives without meaning
All together
Angels watching

One last task to complete
One final road to walk
Caregivers watching
Families watching
Angels watching

Some at peace
Some full of anger
Some wait expectantly
Some wait fearfully
Angels watching

Some know Jesus
Some carry peace
Some carry love
Some carry deep joy
Angels watching

Some follow Satan
Some full of anger
Some full of fear
Some full of hate
Angels watching

All waiting at the doorstep
All ready to cross the threshold
All about to earn their final reward
All unable to turn back
Angels watching

Some full of darkness
Some full of light
Some full of hope
Some full of dread
Angels watching

Which one will I choose?
I choose the light
I choose Jesus
I know my Savior
I know there are angels watching

Which will you choose
Darkness or light
Hatred or love
Unrest or peace
Angels watching

Choose wisely

All cross the final threshold
All will reap their reward

Some go into darkness and despair with anger and fear
Some go into the light with anticipation and joy

Angels are watching

Caregiving

Caregiving Challenges

Sometimes a spouse
Sometimes a sibling
Sometimes a child
Sometimes a more distant relative
Sometimes a friend

Many take on the role of caregiver
Rarely understanding what lies ahead
Willing to sacrifice part of their own life
Willing to put love for another ahead of love of self

Feeling responsible
Feeling scared
Feeling confused
Feeling all alone

Caregiving can mean preparing meals
Caregiving can mean cleaning a home
Caregiving can mean filling a medication planner
Caregiving can be transporting someone to doctors
    appointments

Caregiving can mean bathing your special person
Caregiving can mean dressing your special person
Caregiving can mean walking with, transferring, lifting,
    or turning your special person

Caregiving can mean being an advocate for your
    special person
Caregiving can mean learning medical things in a whole
    new way
Caregiving can mean learning medications you never
    knew existed
Caregiving means interacting with the healthcare system
Caregiving often means financial burden

Satisfaction comes from knowing you are helping your
    special person
Fear comes from questioning your own strength

Often there are sleepless nights
Often your special person does not express gratitude

Sometimes families pull together beautifully
Sometimes families pull apart in ugliness

Hours can seem like days
Days can seem like weeks

Not enough time for everything that needs to be done
Not enough time to just focus on loving your person
Not enough time for your own needs
Too much time spent on another person
Too little time spent on yourself

Stress is high
Exhaustion is high

Caregiving can be brief
Caregiving can be prolonged
Usually not knowing how long

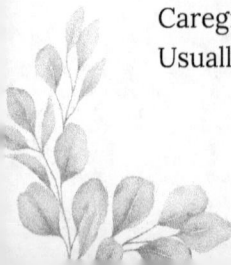

Wondering about your own life
Wondering about your own future
Wondering who will help

Wondering if you can trust anyone
Wondering how you will survive
Wondering what will happen when this chapter closes

Wondering about the meaning of life
Wondering about the meaning of death
Wondering about the meaning of disease and suffering

Searching for answers
Searching for meaning
Searching for rest
Searching for peace
Searching for help

Sometimes "help" looks like a friend
Sometimes "help" looks like a neighbor
Sometimes "help" looks like a church family
Sometimes "help" looks like paid caregivers

Sometimes "help" looks like in-home care
Sometimes "help" looks like a facility
Sometimes "help" looks like hospice

Sometimes "help" is wonderful
Sometimes "help" is frustrating

Where do you turn?

Turn to Jesus
Turn to your heavenly Father
Turn to your Creator
Turn to the only One who has all the answers

The Lord will guide you
The Lord will comfort you
The Lord will strengthen you

The Lord will bring peace in the midst of the storm
The Lord will send angels in disguise

The Lord will send blessings not always immediately seen
The Lord will send provision
The Lord will work in mysterious and wondrous ways

Our systems fail us
Our friends fail us
Our family fails us
Life seems to fail us

But God never fails us
God never abandons us
God never turns His back on us
God loves us
God always loves us

In the midst of suffering
In the midst of hardship
In the midst of trials
In the midst of caregiving
In the midst of dying

There is only God

Draw near to Him now
Lean into Him
Talk to Him
Run to Him
Trust Him

His plans are good
He sees the big picture
He sees the final result

Maybe you have walked closely with the Lord for
    a long time
Maybe you walked closely with the Lord a long time ago
Maybe you have never known what walking closely with
    the Lord is

The Lord wants a relationship with each person
The Lord wants a relationship with you
The Lord wants to hear your thoughts, your feelings,
    your concerns, your questions
The Lord wants you

He wants to be your friend
He wants to be your teacher
He wants to be your guide
He wants to be your comforter
He wants to give you strength

Run to Him
Embrace Him
Cling to Him

Difficult Times

In the Middle of the Storm

Normal, busy, everyday life
Walking, running, the path I'm on
No warning of the storm to come
Running with the Lord
Worried about nothing

Sudden crash
Sudden stop
Unable to breathe
Unable to get back up

Plans changed in an instant
Direction changed in an instant
Paths changed in an instant
Future changed in an instant

Worshiping the Lord before the storm
Worshiping the Lord in the storm
Worshiping the Lord after the storm
Worshiping the Lord regardless of the storm

I rejoiced in the Lord before the storm
I rejoice in the Lord in the middle of the storm
I rejoice in the Lord regardless of the storm
I rejoice in the Lord regardless of the situation

God's love for me isn't dependent on the circumstance
My love for God isn't dependent on the circumstance
God's delight in me isn't dependent on the circumstances
My delight in the Lord isn't dependent on the circumstances

My hope is in the Lord, always
My faith is in the Lord, always
My joy is in the Lord, always
Even in the middle of the storm

Comfort in the Storm

Storms swirl
Winds blow
Floodwaters rise
You keep me safe

Violence abounds
Loss abounds
Grief abounds
You comfort me

Captors appear to win
Heavy chains destroy freedom
Persecution reigns
You stay with me

Mountains all around
Thunderclouds roll in
Cold, hungry, alone
Your loving arms wrap around me

Mountains fall
Chains break
Dark clouds dissipate
You rescued me

Jesus, I worship You
Your face shines more brightly amidst darkness
Your warm gaze is warmest amidst cold
Your love more tender amidst grief and loss

Jesus, You are my everything
Jesus, You destroy hopelessness with hope
Jesus, You are my provider
Jesus, I adore You.

Pain may assault me
But Your love comforts me
Your love casts out fear and despair
Jesus, I worship You.

The hole in my soul is filled
You, Lord, only You
I hunger for You, Jesus
You alone satisfy

Jesus, sweet Jesus
Jesus, all powerful Jesus
Jesus, all knowing Jesus
Jesus, forgiving Jesus

Jesus, I love You
Jesus, I adore You
Jesus, I trust You
Jesus, I worship You

Peace

Rest

I am weary, Lord
I seek Your promised rest
I need Your peace to overwhelm me
I seek Your promised rest

Help me understand resting in You
Help me grow ever closer to You
Help me find Your rest
Help me live the life You have for me

I am still in Your presence, Lord
I am waiting on You, Lord
I am remembering You, Lord
I am seeking more of You, Lord

You are my rock and my salvation
You are my fortress
You are my hope
You are my everything

In You I find rest
In You I find peace
In You anxiety flees
In You fear flees

I run to You, Lord
I run to Your shelter
I run to Your peace
I run to Your rest

You are my rest, Lord

In the midst of the busyness
You are my rest
In the midst of life's chaos
You are my rest

In the midst of life's worries
You are my rest
In the midst of my never-ending to-do list
You are my rest

In the midst of my working
You are my rest
In the midst of suffering
You are my rest

In the midst of life's joys
You are my rest
In the midst of life's sorrows
You are my rest

In the midst of death
You are my rest
In the midst of mourning
You are my rest

I choose to run to You
I choose Your peace
I choose Your rest
I choose You

Truly my soul finds rest in God;
my salvation comes from him.
Truly he is my rock and my salvation;
he is my fortress, I will never be shaken.
Psalm 62:1–2 (NIV)

Peace

You bring peace to my anxious heart
My heartbeat slows as peace descends
I become aware of the soft breeze in my hair
I feel the warmth of the sun's rays

Lord, You take my attention off my worries
I suddenly see the beauty of Your creation
I hear the songs of birds as they sit on tree branches
I feel the blue of the sky overhead

Your peace allows me to notice the rustling leaves
    overhead
Your peace allows me to notice the intricacies of
    Your flowers
Your peace brings forth songs in my heart
Your peace allows me to worship unconstrained

I see the beauty and wonder of Your creation
I see the beauty and wonder of You, Jesus

I see Your majesty
I feel Your love
I know You

I give You my heart
I give You my life
I give You my future
I give You all of me

Your peace descends like light rays
Your peace flows into me
Your peace flows through me

Peace comes because I know You are good
Peace comes because I live in Your light
Peace comes because I gaze upon You
Peace comes because I no longer see the storm

Thank You for Your river of peace
Thank You for giving me rest in Your arms
Thank You for Your peace

Oil of Peace

Peace of God descends like rain
Glittery like gold or silver

Sparkling like diamonds
Like warm oil raining down
Peace
Peace of God

Weighted oil
Heavy oil
Peace
Oil of love

Hustle and bustle all around
Chattering voices abound
But God
God's peace moves not

I surrender all
With surrender comes more peace
More heavenly oil

Peace of God
Oil of God
Oil of love
Peace

His presence palpable
Heavy
On my knees, Lord
On my face, Lord

Oil descending like brilliant diamonds
Warm
Healing
Brilliant
Heavy

More, Lord
More
More presence, Lord,
More oil, Lord
More of You, Lord
More!

My Peace

In the midst of the darkest night
In the midst of the stormiest seas
In the midst of grief
You are my peace

When my heart feels heavy
When my body feels pain
When my soul feels pain
You are my peace

In my brokenness
You are my hope

In my despair
You are my peace

When I feel rejection
You bring acceptance

Friends may betray me
But You are ever faithful

Trust in others may be broken
But You are unshakable

When I am sick
You are my healer

When my heart feels dark
You bring light

In the midst of betrayal
You remain faithful

In the midst of the storm
You extend Your hand of protection

Life's troubles cannot overwhelm me
You alone bring me strength
You alone bring me peace

My heart may be broken
But You restore me

I will keep my eyes on You
I will not look at the storm surrounding me
I will look only upon You

You are my hope
You are my strength
You are my peace

You never leave me
You never forsake me
You never turn against me

I am Your beloved
I am Your child
I am who You say I am

You rescued me
You saved me
You gave me life
You gave me new life

My eyes look to You
My heart is stilled
Your glory chases away all darkness
You are my peace

I will worship You always
I will sing Your praises always
I will glorify You always
You are my peace

Facing Death

Dear Child of Mine
(words from God to those dying)

I am here with you
I am here loving you
I am here waiting for you
I am here with open arms

I long to give you complete forgiveness
I long to give you complete freedom
I long to give you complete healing
I long to give you complete life

Suffering is not from Me
Pain is not from Me
Death is not from Me
Grief is not from Me

I gave My Son to rescue you
I gave My Son to redeem you
I gave My Son to bring you hope
I gave My Son to give you life

I know how hard dying is
I know how hard it is to face suffering
I know how hard it is to let go
I know how hard it is to say goodbye

I am walking with you
I am guiding you
I am carrying you

Give Me your guilt
Give Me your shame
Give Me your regrets

Give Me your pain
Give Me your suffering
Give Me your fears

Come to Me
Come home
Come to your forever home

Come into My peace
Come into My joy
Come into My love

Step into endless peace
Step into endless beauty
Step into endless joy

Come to Me, My child
Come to your Creator
Come

Dying

From conception dying is in our future
Denial runs rampant in our society
People run from death
Yet death is inevitable

Most are too concerned with worldly pleasures of today
Few are concerned with eternity's future
Most believe they control their own destiny
Yet death looms on everyone's horizon

All created for a purpose
All with a plan for their life
All created for relationship
All created for love

All long for love
All long for joy
All long for peace
All long for hope

Only relationship with Jesus brings true love
Only relationship with Jesus brings true joy
Only relationship with Jesus brings true peace
Only relationship with Jesus gives hope, eternal hope

For some seeing death draw near brings fear
For others seeing death draw near brings hope
For some death represents the end of life
For others death represents the birth of new life

For some death represents decay
For others death represents glory
For some death represents the grave
For others death represents going home

I see death as stepping over a threshold
I see death as going home
I see death as stepping into glory
I see death as a reward

What do you see?
What waits for you at death's door?
How do your beliefs impact your future?
How does your future change your present?

End of Life

Life as a youth now long gone
Life as a young adult now a distant memory
Life as a strong independent person lies behind me
Life as I've known it draws near its end

Overwhelming sadness
Overwhelming stress
Overwhelming discouragement

Longing for the life I used to have

I have a deep ache inside
I feel a deep emptiness inside
I feel grief for the losses in my life
I feel confusion amidst the unknown and unfamiliar
I feel fear of what I'm about to walk through

But what is truth?
Truth is what God says about me
What does He say?
He tells me

I am new
I am free
I am loved

I am protected
I am forgiven
I am adopted

I am chosen
I am blessed
I am cherished

I am a child of the Most High
I have an inheritance
I have value
I have a future

I don't need to strive
I can relax
I don't need to be in control
Abba is in control

Failure is a lie from the enemy
Shame comes from the enemy
Condemnation comes from the enemy
Fear comes from the enemy

Truth says I am forgiven
Truth says my repented sins are forgotten
Truth says I am loved
Truth says I am never alone

Sometimes my feelings want to overwhelm me
Sometimes my feelings want to defeat me
Always I need to worship my Lord and King
Always I need to recall what He says over me

Feelings or truth?

Feelings are like quicksand
Truth is the life preserver within reach
I choose to discard feelings
I choose to believe truth

Pain will come
Suffering will come
Death will come
But freedom also comes
Joy also comes

I have hope
I have peace
I have a future

I set aside fear
I set aside loneliness
I set aside despair

Because I have truth
Because I know who I am
Because I know my Creator lives
Because I know my Creator loves

Next Steps

What comes next, Lord?
The path ahead is unlit
Will you turn on the lights, Lord?
Show me what comes next please

Oh, Daughter, do you trust Me?
Yes, Lord, I trust You
I won't show you the whole path ahead
Hold the candle
Take My hand

But, Lord, I might stumble and fall
No, Daughter, not if you hold My hand
But, Lord, how will I see the stumbling blocks and
    mountains ahead?
You don't need to. I do. Trust Me.

Daughter, I want you to trust Me
I want to walk with you by candlelight
I give you enough light to see your next step
You don't need to worry about the mountains ahead
Trust Me.

I remember Your faithfulness, Lord
I remember how You rescued me
I remember how You parted the seas
I remember how You pulled me from the grave
I remember how You gave me life
I remember how You died for me

Jesus, I trust You
Jesus, I thank You
Jesus, I worship You
Jesus, I hold Your hand
Jesus, I follow You

Jesus, the next steps don't matter
Jesus, the stumbling blocks don't matter
Jesus, the mountains don't matter
Jesus, the fires don't matter

Jesus, You are at my side
Jesus, You are my guide
Jesus, You are my light
Jesus, You are my everything
Jesus, my next steps don't matter

Grief

Draw Near to Me

Draw near to Me now, my child
I see your pain
I feel your pain
Draw near to Me now.

Death was never My plan
Satan is the one who steals, kills, and destroys
My arms were open wide to receive your loved one
I did not take them from you

Draw near to Me now, My child
I understand your pain
I'm here to walk with you
I'm here to comfort and strengthen you

Grief is not an easy road to walk
The shadow of death feels overwhelming
I sent My son to rescue all of you
I sent My son to defeat death

Death, where is your sting?
The pain is but a momentary event
Death is not the end
Life is on the other side

Draw near to Me now, My child.
Run to My comforting arms
Feel My love wrapped around you
Hear My heart toward you

Draw near to Me, My child.
I will dry your tears
I will renew your strength
I will always love you

Grief often feels like a dry cactus inside
A dry cactus that draws blood at every turn
But your tears bring new life
Soon the cactus inside will bloom brightly

I will never leave you
I will never forsake you
I will never stop loving you
I will always be here for you

Draw near to Me now, My child
See that My heart is pure love
See that I am your Creator
See that I AM

—God

Psalm of Grief

Father, You are the source of life, the Almighty Creator
I praise You for the breath in my lungs
I praise You for my beating heart
I praise You for the majesty of Your creation

My heart is like a cactus—dry, sharp, drawing blood
    with every turn
The cactus is named Grief
Loss tried to overwhelm me
Pain wants to destroy me

With You, I am less than dust
But You are the river of life
You wash over me and I come to life
The dry cactus begins to bloom

Where there was death there is hope
With hope comes life
Jesus is my hope
Jesus is my life

Thank You, Jesus for restoration, strength and hope
I live because of You
I live for You
I praise You even in the darkness

Sudden Grief

Like a gut punch
First shock
Then waves of nausea
Then tears

Head spinning
Dizziness
Confusion
Pain

Red swollen eyes
Not enough tears
Not enough tissues

Not enough clarity
Not enough hugs
Not enough words

Not enough time
Not enough memories
Not enough togetherness

Headaches
Stomachaches
Heartaches

Grief hits hard
Grief surrounds like dense fog
Grief brings confusion

Waves of grief
Waves of calm
Waves of comfort

Repeat

Uncontrolled weeping
Uncontrolled pain
Uncontrolled grief

But Jesus

Outside the tomb of Lazarus
Jesus wept
Jesus understands
Jesus cares

He calls me to run to Him
His wide open arms beckon
His desire is to comfort
His desire is to heal

Crushed in spirit
I know my Redeemer lives
Crushed today
I know tomorrow I will be healed

I know God's promises are true
I know He promises comfort
I know He promises healing
I know He promises eternity for His children

He says He is close to the brokenhearted
He says one day death will be no more
He promises life
I believe Your word, Lord Jesus

Without you I am lost

I am desperate for You
I choose life over death
I choose gratitude over resentment
I choose joy amidst the tears

Satan comes to steal
Satan comes to kill
Satan comes to destroy

Satan's time is short
Satan will not win
Satan will be destroyed

What Satan meant for harm
The Lord will use for good
Crushed today
Stronger tomorrow

Grief will not overtake my heart of gratitude
Grief will not destroy me
Grief leads to greater compassion
Grief is the price for great love

The Lord is near
The Lord is pure love
The Lord is our true comforter
The Lord never leaves me

I feel Your presence, Lord
I feel Your comfort amidst the pain
I hear You telling me to allow the tears
I hear You tell me to embrace this walk

The tears will stop
The swirling will cease
The fog will lift

Hope remains
Peace remains
Joy remains in the midst of sorrow

Grief erupts from deep below
Peace descends from on high
Heaven and earth collide

I can choose to look down into despair
I can choose to look up to find peace
I can choose to look up to find love
I can choose to look up to find joy

The choice is clear
Choose death?
Or Choose life
I choose life

You don't owe me an explanation
You don't owe me anything
I have nothing without You
I choose to worship You

I choose to worship in the midst of the tears
I choose to worship without understanding
I choose peace, love, and joy.

Praise be to the God and Father of our Lord Jesus Christ,
the Father of compassion and the God of all comfort,
who comforts us in all our troubles,
so that we can comfort those in any trouble
with the comfort we ourselves receive from God.
2 Corinthians 1:3–4 (NIV)

Widowhood

A Widow's Grief

Sudden grief
Unwanted grief
Ugly grief

Stabbing pain
Ripping pain
Nonstop pain

So many whys
So many "if only's"
So many regrets

One life ended
One family changed
My life forever changed

New challenges
New beginnings
New life

First there is shock
First there are tears
First there is brain fog

At first there is busyness
At first there is confusion
At first there are so many decisions

Then comes the unwanted changes
Then comes the loneliness
Then comes the emptiness

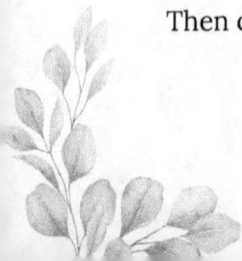

Changes in routines
Changes in families
Changes in friendships

Slowly new life emerges
Slowly the trauma fades
Slowly the pain subsides

New routines
New goals
New life

Birthday memories
Anniversary memories
Holiday memories

Painful memories
Happy memories
Unexpected memories

Feelings of anger
Feelings of loss
Feelings of gratefulness

Grateful for the smiles
Grateful for the laughter
Grateful for the love

Grateful for the first kiss
Grateful for the last kiss
Grateful for all the time in between

Grateful for the sweet memories
Grateful for the shared dreams
Grateful for the shared life

Grateful for my new hope
Grateful for my new dreams
Grateful for my new life

Grateful for my Jesus
Grateful for God's grace
Grateful for God's mercy

Knowing this life is temporary
Knowing there is more
Knowing there is so much more

Learning to find comfort in the arms of Jesus
Learning to hear the voice of our Creator
Learning to know the love of the Father

Now I understand the gift of a spouse
Now I understand the gift of love
Now I understand that love always lives on

Love comes from God
Love never fails
Love never ends

Great grief comes only after great love
Grief does not win
Love wins

Life as a Widow

Sometimes lonely
Sometimes freeing
Sometimes full of memories of days gone by
Sometimes full of dreams of the future
Sometimes full of tears

Life as a widow
Life filled with blessings and not so much blessings
Life sometimes filled with the pain of loss
Life sometimes full of fear of the unknown
Sometimes able to see some of the blessings

Who is wise enough to acknowledge the blessings?
Who is strong enough to appreciate the blessings?

No longer a need to consult another
No longer a need to share a bathroom
No more discussions about finances
No more misunderstandings
No more sleepless nights due to the sound of snoring

Freedom to do what I want when I want

Things which don't feel like blessings include
    things expected, things unexpected

No more hugs
No more holding hands
No more "honey can you help me . . ."
No more laughing at silly jokes only the two of you
    understand

No more sharing joys
No more sharing sorrows
No more help with finances
No more snuggles
No more loving glances

Life as a widow drives you to your knees
Seeking the only true source of love
Seeking the arms of the Father
Feeling the loving gaze of Jesus

Life as a widow forces questioning ones life
Life as a widow makes one aware of strength
    previously unknown
Once my future was intertwined with another
Now intertwined only with the Lord

Life is forever moving from season to season
Life is forever full of new challenges
Life is forever full of new possibilities
Life is forever full of new joys

One thing is certain
Marriage brought great joy
But with Jesus great joy can be found as a widow too
Joy, like a deep well, abounds even amidst sadness
    and loss

Only the Father can make one whole
Only God is perfect love
Thank You, Father, for teaching me about unconditional
    love through marriage
Thank You, Father, for teaching me about Your unconditional
    love through widowhood

I am truly blessed
I thank You, Lord
I thank You for the joy
I thank You for the sorrow
I thank You for life and love

I thank You for what was
I thank You for what is
I thank You for loving me

I thank You for comforting me
I thank You for strengthening me
I thank You for what is to come

Michael, Promising Forever

Brown eyes
Dark brown hair
Dark brown beard

Brown skin
Huge smile
Huge laugh

Gentle
Outgoing
Full of laughter
Playful

Promising forever

Loving
Adoring
Romantic

Bouquets of flowers
Handwritten love notes
Long, sweet kisses

Promising forever

Walking in fallen leaves in autumn
Walking Ginger around the neighborhood
Walking Misfit around the lake
Exercising at the gym

Anniversary getaways
Boating on the lake
Hot tubs and romance

Promising forever

Learning to parent
Building a home
Planting roses
Rescuing cats and dogs

Warm bear hugs
Holding hands
Snuggles
Always smiling

Loving glances
Private jokes
Always laughing

Promising forever

Christmas presents
Birthday presents
Graduation presents
Anniversary presents

Teddy bears
Jewelry
Flowers

Family time
Couple time
Precious time

Promising forever

Semi-trucks
Moving trucks
Concrete trucks

Townhouse
Apartment
Condominium
House

Hand in hand
Two as one

Promising forever

Trips to Tennessee
Trips to Michigan
Trips to Iowa
Trips to Arkansas
Trips to Mississippi

Trips to Hot Springs
Trips to Gulf Shores
Trips to family reunions
Trips unfulfilled

Visiting church
Talking about God
Baptism
Confirmation

Promising forever

Emergency room
Hospital room
Oxygen concentrators
Hospice
Moving to heaven

Promising forever

Michael, you promised to love me forever. You promised
to always be at my side. You didn't choose to leave me.
Thank you for keeping your promise. You left your love
with me. I feel you still beside me. Promising forever.
I will see you in heaven. My heart, my love, is with you,
sweet husband. Forever.

Death of a Child

Dearest Brian

Today I remember you
Today I remember the joy of your birth
Today I remember the horrific day of your death

Fifty-four years ago today
Fifty-four years of remembering your last sound
Fifty-four years of wondering why
Fifty-four years of questions without answers

I remember your tiny hands
I remember your sweet smell
I remember your red hair
I remember your velvet soft skin

I remember promising to always take care of you
I remember the thrill of motherhood
I remember the sound of your cry
I remember the sweet smile on your tiny face

I remember that day you left us
I remember too well
I remember the abnormal sound
I remember the horror of realizing you weren't breathing

I remember the frantic calls for help
I remember the hurried trip to the emergency room
I remember the waiting to hear what I already knew
I remember being sent home with only your clothes

I remember the questions from friends and family
I remember the frustration of not knowing what happened
I remember thinking your death was somehow my fault
I remember leaving the tiny casket at the cemetery

I remember the extreme pain
I remember the complete devastation
But I also remember the good
I also remember how life changed

Your death destroyed the life I had
Your death led to a new life
Your death led to a new purpose
Your death led me to help others

I remember the heartbreak of your death
I remember the many good things coming from it
I remember the words Sudden Infant Death Syndrome
I remember the many unanswered questions

I used to think answers would come
Now I know better
I used to think your death meant the end of my life
Now I know better

Brian, your life was so very short
But your life had so much meaning
Brian, your life and death ended up helping so many people
Brian, thank you for being you

I still don't understand what happened
I still don't understood why healthy babies just die
I still don't understand why babies continue to die
        without explanation
I still don't understand

But I know God uses even hard tragedies for good
I know that so much good can come from what seems
        horrific
I know that God is love
I know that I trust Him

I know that you still live in my heart
I know that you still inspire me to help others
I know that I still feel so blessed to have held you
        in my arms
I know that I truly am blessed

Brian, my son, you may be gone from this realm,
        but you are never forgotten

Love always,
Mommy

Brian, My Son

I remember the sounds of your newborn cry
I remember your sweet baby smell
I remember the feel of your velvet skin
I remember

My child
My baby
My son

So much joy came when you came
So much pain came when you left
So many dreams of your future
So much agony when your life ended

Father, I don't understand
Father, I need You
Father, comfort this momma's broken heart
Father, I trust You

The wounds of your death, Brian, have turned to scars
Scars remind me of you each day
The hope of seeing you in heaven
Sustains me through the years

The fairy-tale life ended so abruptly
But your short life impacted so many
Your birth changed me
Your death broke me
My life ended with yours

Jesus gave me hope
Jesus wrapped His arms around me
Despair replaced with hope

Sorrow replaced with joy
Death turned to life
New life
Different life

Painful memories turn to joyful memories
Moments frozen in time
Cherished memories never far away
Precious moments burned on my heart

Death stole you from me
Death took you way too soon
Your death took my youth
Your death changed my life

New insight
New vision
New life
New gratitude

Thank You, Lord, for life
Thank You, Lord, for restoration
Thank You for comforting me

Thank You, Lord, for strengthening me.
Thank You, Lord, for my sweet son
Thank You, Lord, for the hope of heaven

Brian Alan Schnathorst, September 1–October 8, 1971
Gone, never forgotten.

Then the virgin will rejoice in the dance,
And the young men and the old, together,
For I will turn their mourning into joy
And will comfort them
and give them joy for their sorrow.
Jeremiah 31:13 (NASB 1995)

Hospice Nursing

Called

I've called you
I've called you to step out of your comfort zone
I've called you to say and do things you don't think
    are possible
I've called you to lean into My ways

I have more plans for you
Each moment of your life has purpose
I want to use you more
I've called you to be a light

Bring light into the darkness
Bring truth where others only know lies
Bring My love to all people
Bring hope to all people

Show others My love
Show others My goodness
Show others My mercy
Show others how to follow Me

When you are weary, come to Me
When you are weary I will give you strength
When you feel suffering, give it to Me
When you feel suffering, I will give you comfort

Do you feel anxious? Let go of the fear
Do you feel hopeless? I am the definition of hope
Do you feel weak? I am your strength
Do you feel confused? I am the author of your life

My child, I love you
My child, I cherish you
My child, follow Me
My child, trust Me

My child, I love you
Oh, how I love you!
My beloved child!

I love to watch you
I love to be with you
I love to hear your voice
I love dancing with you

I love you for you
I adore you
I delight in you
I love engaging with you

I am yours
You are Mine

I love you
Oh, how I love you!
My beloved child!

I am the answer to everything for you
I am the answer to all your wants
I am the answer to all your needs
I am the answer

I am here for you always
I love you always
Darling child of Mine.

—God

Nursing

Once walked away from
Once taken back up
Once taken from me

Called to lay it down
Called to pick it up
Called into a new field

Questioning competency
Questioning stamina
Questioning direction

Stepping out of the boat
Stepping out in faith
Stepping out without answers

Jesus, I listen for Your voice
Holy Spirit, I follow Your lead
Father, I trust You

You are rewriting my history
Destiny is straight ahead
Past mistakes made right

Born again creation
Cleansed by the blood
Brand-new creation

Doubts gone
Fears gone
Past mistakes gone

Lord, You are good
Lord, You are faithful
Lord, You are pure love

Lord, You called me to hospice
Lord, I know of Your goodness
Lord, I know You are never going to let me down

New life awaits
New challenges await
New blessings await

Reflections of a Hospice Nurse

Sick people
Hurting people
Frightened people
Angry people
Dying people

Families of dying people
Scared families
Confused families
Angry families
Grieving families

Hospice nurses come to help
Hospice nurses come to bring comfort
Hospice nurses come to ease the suffering
Hospice nurses come to bring hope
Hospice nurses come to bring peace

Anxious and depressed patients
Anxious and depressed families
Grieving patients
Grieving families
Grieving hospice nurses too

Nurses assess
Nurses treat wounds
Nurses treat pain
Nurses treat symptoms
Nurses document

Patients' pain and suffering are real
Nurses see it all
Nurses hear it all
Nurses feel it all
Nurses carry it all

Hospice nurses learn about lives lived
Hospice nurses learn about past mistakes
Hospice nurses learn of great accomplishments
Hospice nurses learn of great tragedies
Hospice nurses learn of great strengths

Hospice nurses go from patient to patient
Hospice nurses go from family to family
Hospice nurses go from home to home
Hospice nurses go from facility to facility
Hospice nurses go from county to county

Patients lean on nurses
Families lean on nurses
Facilities lean on nurses
The burden is heavy
The burden is hard

Critical thinking a must
Problem solving a must
Compassion a must
Resilience a must
Grief is inevitable

Amidst the suffering, hospice nurses bring smiles
Amidst the suffering, hospice nurses bring love
Amidst the suffering, hospice nurses bring peace
Sometimes hospice nurses even bring joy
Amidst the suffering, hospice nurses give their all

Hospice nurses sacrifice their time to help others
Hospice nurses sacrifice their talents to help others
Hospice nurses sacrifice their own safety to help others
Hospice nurses sacrifice their own resources to help others
Hospice nurses sacrifice themselves to help others

The joy comes sporadically
The joy comes from knowing they've made a difference
The joy comes from weak smiles
The joy comes from warm hugs
The joy comes from seeing lives lived fully

Death comes to our patients
Death changes their families
Death changes their communities
Death changes their nurses
Death hurts them all

But death is not the end
Death is a new beginning
Death brings birth
Death does not eliminate a life
Death does not win

I know my Creator is love
I know my Creator is forgiving
I know my Creator knows each of us
I know my Creator understands
I know my Creator. Do you?

The pain is real
The burden of grief is real
Pain, suffering, and grief are not meant to be
    borne alone
Pain, suffering, and grief are meant to be given
    to our Lord
The burden is meant to be shared

I am a hospice nurse
I have the privilege of helping people
I have the privilege of entering the lives of others
I have the privilege of loving people in a special way
I have the privilege of walking people home

Sometimes I feel great satisfaction
Sometimes I feel overwhelmed
Sometimes I feel like throwing up
Sometimes I feel like screaming
Sometimes I have to cry

Tears are not a bad thing
Tears wash away the pain
Tears water seeds planted
Tears lead to new growth
Tears lead to new life

Sometimes my heart is troubled
Sometimes my heart is burdened
Sometimes my heart is filled with peace
Sometimes my heart is filled with joy
Always my heart is filled with my Lord

The burden is too great to carry alone
The grief is too much to bear alone
Thank You, Father, for strengthening me
Thank You, Father, for taking this burden from me

Thank You, Father, for each precious patient
Thank You, Father, for each precious family
Thank You, Father, for each precious memory
Thank You, Father, for the privilege and honor
        of working as a hospice nurse

Life as a Nurse Care Manager

In the beginning:

Written names
Unknown faces
Faces of illness
Faces of fear
Faces of sadness
Faces of loss
Suddenly faces full of smiles
Big, beautiful, priceless smiles

Mistrust to trust
Handshakes to hugs
Uncertainty to enthusiasm
Tears to laughter
Stranger to friend
Trepidation to love, to joy

Long drives
Breathless beauty
Treacherous walks
Thunderstorms
Snowstorms
Ice storms

Extreme heat
Extreme cold
Extreme wealth
Extreme poverty

Extreme blessings
Extreme danger
Nonstop phone calls
Nonstop needs
Endless charting

In the end:

Loss
Sudden
Painful
Overwhelming
Tears, this time mine
Grief, this time mine
Gut-wrenching grief

Repeat.

In memory and honor of all those in my care.
Never forgotten.

Shadows

We have cared for many patients
We have lost many of our patients
Knowing their end was near
It still hurt when they left

Grief is for families
Grief is for lifelong friends
Yet grief hits caregivers too
Grief is never easy

Memories of those who have gone
Faces of those gone
Voices of those gone
Lives suddenly changed

Like a mist that lingers
Faint but ever present
Like a feather brushing across one's face

Difficult to articulate
A vague awareness
A gut feeling

They were here yesterday
They are gone today

Real connections
Broken by loss

Yet there is a lingering
Like a cool penetrating mist
Unable to grasp
Palpable and impactful

Is this only a memory?
Is this a part of them left behind?
Part of their essence, their energy, their spirit left behind?

Is this a gift or a curse?
Is it bringing uneasiness or bringing peace and comfort?
We get to choose
Choose peace and comfort

Walking with those dying
Spending time with those in between worlds
Pulled away from our day to day existence
Glimmers of what is to come

Shadows that follow us
Shadows that extend our reach
Shadows only sometimes visible yet ever present

What lingers behind is seared on my heart
I am forever changed by each one
It's a gift, a precious gift
A gift that shapes me, guides me

Past interactions with those now gone
Prepare for interactions present and future
Although gone in the physical
Their legacy remains

All are intertwined
Part of something bigger
Part of something beautiful
Part of something amazing

We are all part of God's masterpiece
We see the tangled underside of an elaborate embroidery
God sees the incredibly beautiful masterpiece from above

Take heart

Don't let loss stop you
Don't be afraid of keeping part of them with you

The shadows aren't here to harm
The shadows are here to guide
The shadows can give us wisdom

God's plan is ever present
Each of us has purpose
Each of us is loved and cherished by our Creator

Let us continue to walk forward
Lending helping hands wherever we can
Let us be grateful for the lives we have touched
Let us be grateful for the shadows

Let us support one another
Let us help one another
Let us move forward together
Let us move forward in strength and purpose
Let us embrace the shadows that stay with us

Four Visits as a Hospice Nurse

First patient asleep upon arrival
First patient always confused
First patient aggressive in the past
First patient unpredictable
First patient always a challenge

First patient opens her eyes
First patient flashes a huge smile
First patient with bright sparkling blue eyes
First patient speaks only in a whisper
First patient tells me she loves me

Second patient much newer
Second patient smiles in delight seeing "her" nurse
Second patient also confused

Second patient thanks me for coming
Second patient starts dancing to the music with me
Second patient hugs me and tells me she loves me (CC)

Third patient asleep upon arrival
Third patient curled up in a fetal position
Third patient opens her eyes
Third patient smiles in recognition

Fourth patient visit his last
Fourth patient lying in his casket
Fourth patient now a treasured memory
Fourth patient family now the focus

Hugs and thank you's from wife and daughter
"I love you's" from wife and daughter
Tears of sadness flow from each
Tears of gratitude flow from each

End of day means another long drive
Severe storms abound
Tornado sirens sound
Home to chart
Just another day as a home hospice nurse

Losing Another Patient

Another beloved patient gone
Once again the hurt inside defies words

I've walked hand in hand with each one
I've smiled with them
I've laughed with them
I've prayed with them

I've guided them
I've educated them
I've prayed over them
I've prayed with them

I've brought smiles
I've brought comfort
I've brought hope
I've brought love

I've taught family
I've encouraged family
I've helped restore family
I've cried with family

I'm supposed to be the strong one
I'm supposed to be the one others lean on
I'm supposed to act professional
I'm supposed to deny my own feelings

But my pain is real
My tears are real

The pain inside is intense
The pain inside isn't unexpected
But the pain inside still makes me reel

Lord, why do You want me to do this thing called
    hospice nursing?
Lord, can't You see I'm too weak?
Can't You see I care too much?
Can't You see this repetitive grief is too much?

Oh, dear child of Mine
Why do you think I chose you?

I chose you to be My hands and feet
I chose you to love on the dying as I love them
I chose you because you feel the pain

I chose you because you care
I chose you because I know you will love them
I chose you because I know you will comfort them

You love from a human perspective
I love from an eternal perspective
I chose you to guide them home to Me

I know it hurts you when they pass
I know your grief is real
I know your love for them is real

I did not promise this would be an easy job
I promised to use you for My will

I promise to greet you with open, loving arms
Run to Me
I promise to carry the burden of grief
Give it to Me

It's okay to pull back for a bit
It's okay to shed tears for a bit
It's okay to withdraw for a bit

Run to Me and I will give you strength
Run to Me and I will give you peace
Run to Me and I will restore your joy
Run to Me and give Me the burden of grief

I never asked you to carry this burden alone
I never asked you to serve them alone
I asked you to give your burden to Me
I asked you to serve them with Me

Keep on serving
Don't give up
Keep on loving
Keep on turning to Me

Hospice On Call Night

Two women
One young
One old
Both dying

One in a private home
Surrounded by family
Struggling to die
Fighting to live

One in a care center
Around the clock care
Longing for death
Yet showing signs of improvement

The young woman on daily visits
Her death is imminent
No longer eating
No longer drinking
No longer conscious

The older woman seems well
Eating better
Drinking regularly
No one concerned
No one suspecting

Middle of the night phone call
On call hospice nurse expectant
Anticipating a death call
Anticipating the young woman's passing

The death call comes
Not as anticipated
Older woman found dead
Died in her sleep
All are shocked

Waiting for family
Waiting to support those grieving
Time for thoughts
Time for reflection

Both women are Christian
Both women are married
Both women on hospice
Both at the end of their lives

Which is better I wonder
The older spent her last days living
The younger spent her last days dying
The older died alone in her bed
The younger had family with her

Why does death come quickly to some?
Why does death linger for others?

Why do some suffer immeasurably?
Why do others get spared?

Why do some die young?
Why do some die old?

Why?

Walking beside those who are dying
Walking beside those who are grieving
The darkness is heavy
The grief is heavy

Each birth is unique
Each life lived is unique
Each death is unique

Some fast
Some slow
Each with highs and lows

Each life filled with purpose
Each life filled with meaning
Each life filled with impact

Family arrives
Walking husband and daughter to the room
Helping family cope
Calling the funeral home
Saying final goodbyes
Attempting to provide words of comfort

Second call comes
Second death call
Younger woman's death

Take a deep breath
There is much more to do
God is with you
God will strengthen you

Long drive
Dark night
Middle of the night
Eerie sense of calm

Arrive at the home
Husband and daughters present
Another lifeless body
Another family filled with grief

Verify death
Offer condolences

Call the doctor
Call the coroner
Call the funeral home

Console the husband
Console the daughters
Console the dog

Count narcotics
Destroy narcotics
Sign paperwork
Remove equipment

The business ends
Time to leave
Final condolences
Final goodbyes

Into the dark night
Onto the dark highway
Long drive home

Tired
Exhausted
Reflective
Grateful

Grateful for each life
Grateful for the opportunity to serve
Grateful for being able to help
Grateful for being able to bring comfort
Grateful for being a hospice nurse

Grateful to arrive home
Grateful for my own life
Grateful for a little sleep
Grateful for the many patients I have yet to meet
Grateful to be able to start all over again

Home Hospice Nurse Musings

Men and women
Some young
Some old

Some in mansions
Some in poverty
End of life for each of them

Some have loving family
Some are so very alone
Some are frightened

Some are accepting
Some are suffering
Some are at peace

All at the end of their life

Busy freeways
Lonely back roads
Rush hour traffic

Heat waves
Cold waves

Thunderstorms
Snowstorms
Ice storms

Long drives to patients

Undeterred by weather
Undeterred by bad roads
Undeterred by heavy traffic

Hugs from grateful patients and caregivers
Harsh words from angry, frightened people

Some feel the blessings
Some only feel anger

All facing end of life

Each walks into the sunset
The sunset of their lives
Some are prepared
Many are not

Age is not a factor.
Wealth is not a factor
Career is not a factor

Home is not a factor
Location is not a factor
Status is not a factor

Life gets simpler at end of life
Love looks different at end of life
Success looks different at end of life
Hope looks different at end of life
Faith looks different at end of life

Smiles matter
Handshakes matter
Hugs matter
Caring matters

Hope matters
Love matters
Prayer matters
Peace matters

Going home
Home to their Creator

I am a home hospice nurse
I walk with these patients
I walk with their caregivers

I walk through darkness
I bring the light
I kick out fear

I alleviate suffering when I'm able to
I decrease anxiety wherever I go
I carry peace with me
I carry the fragrance of Jesus with me

I assess
I listen
I communicate
I intervene
I educate

I coordinate
I comfort
I care
I pray
I love

I am a home hospice nurse

I travel from home to home
I take care of details
I ponder the meaning of life

I walk people home

What a challenge to walk people home
What a privilege to walk people home
What an honor to walk people home

Thank You, Father, for Your grace and mercy
Thank You, Father, for Your endless love
Thank You, Father, for home hospice nursing

A Hard Week as Hospice Nurse

Unending pain
Unending trauma
Unending suffering
Unending grief

How do I keep going
How do I keep on smiling
How do I keep encouraging
How do I know how best to intervene

How do I shine love
How do I bring hope to the hopeless
How do I bring comfort to those in pain
How do I help the hurting

Alone I can do nothing
Alone I despair
Alone I become hopeless
Alone I suffer with them

But You, Lord

You and only You understand
You, only You, can heal the broken
You, only You, bring hope to the hopeless
You, only You, bring life to the lifeless

I can do nothing without You, Lord

I can never be good enough
I can never be smart enough
I can never be wise enough
I can never be strong enough

In the presence of patients I show strength
In the presence of my patients I show confidence
In the presence of my patients I show love
In the presence of my patients I show understanding

Away from my patients I feel unimaginable heartbreak
Away from my patients I feel unimaginable pain
Away from my patients I feel unimaginable grief
Away from my patients I feel unimaginable trauma

But You, Lord

You wrap Your arms around me
You wipe my tears
You give me rest
You renew my spirit

I cry out to You
This is too hard!
This is too heavy!
This hurts too much!

You respond

Give it to Me, dear child
Give Me your pain
Give Me your grief
Give Me your weary heart

You only see the pain in front of you
You only see the grief in front of you
You only see the present

When you are overwhelmed by what you see
When you are overwhelmed by what you hear
When you are overwhelmed by what you feel

Turn your eyes toward Me
Turn your ears toward My Word
Turn your feelings toward My love

You fail to see the big picture
You fail to see My eternal plan of love
You fail to see Me in your midst

Dry your tears, My child
Cloak yourself in My armor
Get up and stand tall, My child
Stop trying to use your strength
Use My strength instead

You see much
I see more
You feel much
I feel more
You understand little
I understand all

I am with you in the fire
I am with you in the pain
I am with you in the suffering
I am with you in the grief

Jesus experienced pain
Jesus experienced suffering
Jesus experienced grief
Jesus experienced triumph

It's okay to shed tears
The tragedies you witness are hard to witness
The cries of pain you hear are hard to hear
Few see and hear what you see and hear
Consider it a gift for it gives you wisdom

I choose to use you because you care
I choose to use you because your love is real
I choose you to shine Jesus in the midst of the tragedies
I choose you to serve as I have served

Serve in My strength
Serve in My peace
Serve in My love
Serve in My hope

Share My strength
Share My peace
Share My love
Share My hope

Have Your Way, Lord

As I touch the lives of others
Have Your way
As I touch those in pain
Have Your way

Emotional trauma
Physical trauma
Spiritual trauma
Only You are healer

Broken minds
Broken spirits
Broken bodies
Only You are healer

Have Your way, Lord

Bring peace to those in need
Bring comfort to those in pain
Bring hope to the hopeless

Have Your way, Lord

Restore broken relationships
Restore lost faith
Restore lost lives

Bring salvation to the lost
Bring righteousness to the unrighteous
Bring holiness to the unholy

Have Your way, Lord

Lord, I give You my life
Lord, use me to shine Your love
Lord, have Your way in me

Let me shine light everywhere I go
Let me shine love in all I say
Let me shine light in all I do

Have Your way, Lord

Let others see You in me
Let others feel Your love through me
Let others find hope through me

May my words turn into Your words
May my actions turn into Your actions
May my life become more like Your life

Have Your way, Lord

Patient Stories

Who Do You See?

One tiny frail woman
Living in a long-term care facility
One tiny woman
Consumed by Alzheimer's

Once a strong farmer's wife
Once a young mother
Once helping in the schools
Once active in her church

Once an accomplished seamstress
Once a willing volunteer in her community
Once respected and admired
Once a woman with dignity

Now isolates in one room
Now her mind confused
Now frequently overcome with fear
Now frequently aggressive

The noise outside her room is often deafening
Other patients calling out, yelling, some crying
Many footsteps of employees going back and forth
      outside her door
The noise worsens the confusion

I see a woman in despair
I see total hopelessness
I see a woman suffering
I see a woman betrayed

I see a woman with many people nearby
I see a woman totally alone

Choosing a care center to provide care
Finding loss of freedom
Finding loss of hope
Finding loss of control
Finding complete loss of self

Is this a home or a prison?
Is this what years of saving for becomes?
Where is her dignity?
Where is her peace?

What is the answer?

I know Jesus is always the answer
I know Jesus is pure love
I know Jesus is all powerful

There is power in the name of Jesus
There is freedom in the name of Jesus

Lord, how do I help her and others like her?

Lord, You have put this woman's plight on my heart

There is purpose in the pain
Show me Your purpose
Show me Your plan
Show me how to intervene

Show me how to be like Jesus

Break the chains that imprison her
Speak the name of Jesus
Pray over her
Call out His name

Cast out fear
Cast out confusion
Cast out chaos
Cast out evil

Usher in peace
Usher in hope
Demonstrate love
Demonstrate compassion

Show her Jesus

Get others to pray
Get others aware
Get others united in prayer

Pray for freedom from confusion
Pray for freedom from insensitive care
Pray for freedom.from demonic attack

Pray for caregivers to understand the meaning of care
Pray for caregivers to learn compassion
Pray for the light of Jesus to bring hope in darkness

Thank You, Lord, for showing me how to help
Thank You, Lord, for showing me how to help give her
    purpose again
Thank You, Lord, for showing me how to see her
    smiles again
Thank You, Lord, for showing me how to see her
    joy return
Thank You, Lord, for answered prayers

The Man with a Past

Lonely old man
Tied to an oxygen machine
Lungs wearing out
Heart wearing out
Body wearing out

Still full of spunk
Still full of stories
Still full of life
Still full of hope for something more

One trip to the hospital
Grim test results
Big medical terms
All say death is approaching

Home hospice care begins
No religion
No chaplain allowed
No connection to his children
Living all alone

Hospice nurse sent to help
Help with symptoms
Help with medications
Help with pain management
Help prepare for death

Hospice nurse arrives to serve
Hospice nurse who follows Jesus
Hospice nurse willing to listen
Hospice nurse willing to acknowledge religion hurt
Hospice nurse willing to hear life stories

Stories of multiple marriages
Stories of multiple children and grandchildren
Stories of serving in the military
Stories of battling alcohol
Stories of pain and suffering

Emotional walls gradually come down
Emotional trust gradually built
Emotional vulnerability gradually increased
Emotional trauma revealed eventually

Cut off from family due to past mistakes
Cut off from family due to harm committed to his children
Cut off from family due to harm committed to his
    grandchildren
Cut off from family due to shame and regret

Hospice nurse willing to share testimony
Hospice nurse willing to be vulnerable
Hospice nurse willing to show compassion
Hospice nurse willing to show love

No preaching
No Bible thumping
No judgment
No condemnation

Caring
Compassion
Concern
Commitment

Sharing the love of Jesus
Showing the love of Jesus
Leading to the arms of Jesus
Leading from darkness into light
Leading into peace

Death drawing ever nearer
Family decide to visit one last time
Family struggling with past trauma
Family struggling with unforgiveness

Hospice nurse called to meet with family and patient
Hospice nurse spoke on the power of forgiveness
Hospice nurse shared the good news of Jesus
Hospice nurse witnessed forgiveness replacing anger

Relationships begin to be built
Relationship between the patient and his Creator
Relationship between the patient and his children
Relationship between the patient and his grandchildren

Death comes as death does
Death brings grief
Death also brings gratitude for peace
Death is never the end

Funeral service brought friends and family together
Family invites hospice nurse to come
Family invites hospice nurse to speak
Family invites hospice nurse to share truth

Hospice nurse speaks at funeral
Hospice nurse shares testimony
Hospice nurse shares love of Jesus
Hospice nurse shows love

Family and friends find hope
Family and friends find peace
Family and friends find Jesus
Family and friends will never forget

Young military men in dress uniform in attendance
Young military men there to give honor
Young military men heard that testimony
Young military men share their lives are forever changed
    by what they heard

Remember the man on the cross next to Jesus?
Remember he hadn't memorized the Bible?
Remember he hadn't been baptized?
Remember he was saved anyway?

If the heart still beats
If the lungs still breathe
If the brain can still process
If a person is still able to make a choice

It's not too late

It's not too late for a sinner to be saved
It's not too late to cast out darkness
It's not too late to usher in light

It's not too late to show someone love
It's not too late to exchange death for life
It's not too late to experience true love

It's not too late

Everlasting life
True life
True purpose
True meaning

Never underestimate the power of love
Never underestimate the power of ones testimony
Never underestimate the power of truth
Never underestimate the power of the Holy Spirit
    working through you

Maria

Maria, seventy years old, lifeless in her bed
Family all around her
Small smile and look of peace on her face
Rosary wrapped around her wrist

Check for breathing
Check for heartbeat
Check for nonreactive pupils
Call time of death

Hugs and condolences to family members
Phone call to the doctor
Phone call to the medical examiner
Phone call to the funeral home

Crowded tiny room
Poor neighborhood
Broken down home
Flies abound

Her wealth, her family
Husband, children, grandchildren galore
Outside children play
Laughter abounds

Adults somber
Adults tearful
Adults surround Maria
Children run in and out

Hispanic family
Only two speak English
Communication happens nonverbally
Compassion overcomes the language barrier

Preparing body for transport
Preparing room for gurney
Family members stream by giving goodbye kisses
Tears and sobs of grief abound

Following Maria to the waiting hearse
Praying for peace and comfort to fall
Praying for strength
Praying for all to have such a wealth of love

I leave this home different from when I arrived
My heart hurts
My tears flow
I am forever impacted by this family

I praise the Lord in life
I praise the Lord in death
I praise the Lord in all things
I praise the Lord for the life of Maria

My flesh longs to hide in bed
My spirit longs to worship
I must choose how to respond
I choose to worship the Lord, Creator of all!

Lord, I surrender all
Lord, I surrender their grief
Lord, I surrender their pain
Lord, I surrender my own desires

The Clinging Hand

Lover of knowledge
Lover of horses
Lover of dogs

Lover of nature
Lover of family
Lover of control

Riddled with cancer
He fought that battle hard
Increasing physical limitations
He fought that battle hard

Questions about the future
Questions about symptoms
Questions about God
Questions, lots of questions

Daughter speaks Jesus
Caregiver speaks Jesus
Hospice nurse speaks Jesus
All show the love of Jesus

Accepting Jesus
Struggling with relationship
Accepting the inevitable
Struggling with pain

Many last wishes
Some met
Some unable to be met
Some partially met

A trip to see horses
A ride in a hot-air balloon
A trip to see old friends
A comfortable, peaceful death

Horses came to him like an old friend
Animals came to him like a family member
One wish fulfilled

A trip to see old friends
Replaced by a video chat
Second partially met

Hot-air ballon ride explored
No longer safe to proceed
One wish unable to be met

Cancer spreading
Pain increasing
Disease progressing
Death drawing nearer

Medications increased
Medications tweaked
Medications changed
Comfort achieved

Search for meaning
Following Jesus
Praying with hospice nurse
Gripping, clinging to her hand
The unspoken "Don't leave me"

Nurse reassures him
"It's okay to stop fighting"
"It's okay to let go"
"It's okay to run to Jesus"

Relaxation comes
Sleep comes
Unconsciousness comes
Peace comes
Death comes

A comfortable death achieved
A peaceful death achieved
One more wish fulfilled

A legacy left behind
Living life to the fullest
Never to be forgotten

His zest for life
His passion in life
His strength of being
His hand clinging tightly to his hospice nurse

Woman with Dementia

Once known as young and strong
Once known as a lover of children
Once known as a community leader
Once a devoted wife and mother

Lewy body dementia steals slowly but surely
Caregiver now needing care
Long-term care facility
Continued decline

Hospice care began
I have the honor of being her nurse
A couple of years older than me
A reminder of the fragility of life

Dementia obvious
Confusion
Disorientation
Challenging behaviors

Sometimes greeted with a smile
Sometimes greeted with a loud outburst
Sometimes ignored
Sometimes hit or spit upon

Slowly she is more accepting
Slowly she greets me with a smile
Slowly she greets me with a laugh

Slowly I am accepted
Slowly I am met with a smile and a giggle
Slowly

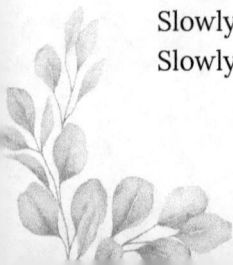

Slowly I get to know this patient
Not as a patient but as a person
Slowly I get to know her devoted daughter
Slowly I get to know her devoted husband

Decline
Changes in eating
Changes in swallowing
Changes in mobility
Slow decline

Slow decline speeding up
Many falls
Unintelligible speech
Devoted daughter
Devoted husband

Praying for my patient
Praying for her family
Praying for her caregivers
Praying for wisdom
Praying for peace

Decline accelerates
The end draws near
Difficult discussions
Difficult decisions

Traumatized husband
Traumatized daughter
Traumatized staff
Traumatized hospice nurse

Preparing for the final days
Preparing for the end
Preparing
Never really prepared

The end comes peacefully
Loss
Heartache
Grief
Memories

Honoring the life that was
Honoring the family that was
Honoring the memory
Honoring the love she gave

Remembering
The good
The difficult
The painful

The moments of joy
The moments of laughter
The moments of tears
Remembering

Wife
Mother
My patient
Forever loved
Forever remembered

The Man Who Loved Cardinals

Beautiful soft brown eyes
Intact brown hair
Joyous laughter
Bright smile

Cardinals fan in all ways
Cardinals sports fan
Red cardinal paintings on his walls
Cardinals shirts and sweaters

Came on hospice
Horrible sores on legs
Failing fast
Ready to leave this world

Questioning his salvation
Convinced he was being punished
Convinced he was unlovable
Lies from the enemy all

Reassuring Bible verses shared
Encouraging prayers shared
Needing physical care
Needing spiritual care

Wonderful daughter
Heartbroken daughter
Struggling to accept illness
Struggling to accept dying

Uncontrollable symptoms
Traumatic for this gentle man
Traumatic for his devoted daughter
Traumatic for all providing care

Hours trying to bring comfort
Hours trying to usher in peace
Hours trying to cast out pain
Hours trying to cast out fear

At last comfort was achieved
At last peace ruled
In time came the last breath
In time this gentle spirit was released

Grieving daughter
Grateful daughter
Thoughtful daughter

Words of gratitude from family
Special gift for his nurse
Two cardinal paintings
Once hung in his room

Now this nurse hangs those cardinals
An ever present reminder
The precious life now passed
The impact never forgotten

Epitaph

Last Words

Sad little girl
Broken little girl
Abused little girl
Lost little girl

Woman crushed with broken promises
Woman crushed with broken trust
Woman crushed with broken hopes
Woman crushed with broken dreams

Woman crushed with grief
Woman crushed with sorrow
Woman crushed with regrets

Born-again woman
Body now old and wrinkled
Finding love with Jesus
Finding pure, perfect love
Old body with a child's spirit

Little girl wonder
Little girl joys
Little girls excitement
Little girl hopes
Little girl dreams

Born-again woman
Born-again child
Born-again life

Sins washed away
Regrets washed away
Grief washed away
Pain washed away

Brand-new life
Joy-filled life
Love-filled life

Sunrise
Sunset
New birth
Old age

Just a dash in between

Joy-filled life
Adventure-filled life
Love-filled life
Hope-filled life

New joy
New adventure
New love
New hope

Clothed in fear for decades
Clothed in depression for decades
Clothed in joy for the rest of eternity
Joyous, miraculous transformation!

Pure peace
Pure joy
Pure love

Dancing in flower-filled fields
Flying high over mountains
Flying with eagles to touch the clouds

Life at its close
Tasks completed
Flying with angels
Dancing with Jesus

Light shines on me
Light shines through me
Light shines from me

Once crushed by life's tragedies
Now exalted on angels' wings
Once in utter despair
Now in pure joy

Come join me, won't you please?
The celebration has just begun
The doors are open for you

If there's breath in your lungs it's not too late
There's a place set that's waiting for you at the table
The master has a robe and a ring waiting for you

Shed no tears at my passing
I have just traveled ahead of you
Rejoice for the love shared
Rejoice for the memories made

I've exchanged my old, broken down body for a new one
My wrinkles are gone forever
My physical struggles are gone forever
Now I dance and fly at will
All my cares have departed

One day your body will grow old
One day your turn will come
Then come join me, won't you please?
Like our Father, my arms will be wide open

My body has come to its end
My spirit lives forever
My love lives forever

My Father is your Father
My Jesus is your Jesus
My joy can be your joy
My future can be your future

Come join me, won't you please?

Follow Jesus
Give Him your life
He gave His to save you

Take the narrow path
There's treasure waiting at the end
Everlasting life awaits
The Father awaits
I await

My love is with you
Always and forever
No matter what

Now celebrate
Hell lost another one
I am free

www.ingramcontent.com/pod-product-compliance
Lightning Source LLC
LaVergne TN
LVHW051414080426
835508LV00022B/3084